If Only I Could Have Said Good-bye

TIM LAMBERT

ISBN:1974141926
ISBN-13:978-1974141920

DEDICATION

This book is dedicated to all the parents who have had to deal with the death of their child. My hope is that you will take something from this book to help you in your own journey.

CONTENTS

TIM LAMBERT

ACKNOWLEDGMENTS

I would like to first thank God for putting this vision in my heart to write this book. I would like to thank my grandmother (Edith) for giving me the approval to write this book and taking the time to answer questions that I had. Thirdly, I would like to thank my mother for passing these stories down to me when I was young and providing me with additional information to write this book. I would also like to thank my Uncle Reginald Roe, Uncle Robert Roe Jr, my wife, Cindy and my two children, Rebekah and Aaron. Thank-you also Beth Turner and Nola Campbell for becoming special friends to my grandmother.

INTRODUCTION

We all have a story. What is the story of your life? What do you want people to remember you by? I sometimes think about these questions in regard to my own life.

This is a story about my grandmother's pain and her resilience with it. My grandmother's life was spent helping others. If her story can help you in anyway, then the purpose of this book has been achieved.

This is a book about grief. It is my grandmother's grief that she experienced after losing four of her sons. It is also a story about coping with it. The loss of your child is a grief I hope to never experience. Just the thought of it brings tears to my eyes. My heart drops when I hear about the death of a child. I imagine yours does also. This is not something any parent wants to go through.

On a family trip to Sister Bay, Wisconsin, I couldn't help to observe the calm water and beautiful sunset that was overlooking the balcony of the place we were staying at. The next day everything was different. There were clouds, rain, and waves crashing the beach. It made me think about grief. With grief you will have times where it may be calm and times where the waves are crashing and almost unbearable. All you can do is learn how to paddle your boat through it. The journey does seem more bearable though when you allow others in the boat with you, such as God, and the people who support you the most.

As a licensed Professional Counselor I have had the opportunity to counsel people in their grief. They have allowed me into their boat. I have seen their tears. I have also seen them find some healing.

I will take some of the things I have learned, as well as things learned from my grandmother, to help you in your own journey through grief.

1 A SOUTHERN GIRL FROM LEXINGTON COUNTY

Edythe Welbourne Bowles was born in Lexington County in the township of Bull Swamp, South Carolina, on February 7, 1922. Her parents were Jasper and Estelle (Lottie) Bowles. She was the sixth child of Lottie's. This was Lottie's second marriage. Lottie had three children by her first husband, William Steele; William Jr, Lila, and Bernice. Lottie and Jasper had three children together; Edythe, Reginald (also called Buck), and Ruth. Very few people knew Edythe's middle name, Welbourne. It was a name that she did not like. Her sister, Bernice, was in nursing school at the time of her birth and there was a doctor that she thought highly of who had the last name of Welbourne. Bernice got her wish. Edythe also did not like the spelling of her first name and would eventually change the spelling to "Edith."

Edith was diagnosed with pneumonia when she was just one year old. At the same time, her father Jasper was ill with congestive heart failure. Bernice was called home to help care for Edith while her mother cared for her father. Edith survived; however, her father did not. Jasper died on February 21, 1923. Life became very tough for Lottie after Jasper's death. There was no income. She would have to make a tough decision that no parent wants to make. She would have to place her children in other homes. Reginald and Ruth were placed in a Lutheran home in

Columbia, South Carolina. Edith; however, was too young for the home. She was sent to live with her sister, Lila, in Springfield, South Carolina. Lila and her husband treated Edith very well. Lila had children of her own that Edith played with. Even though she felt loved, she always felt as though she did not fit in. It wasn't the same as being at home with her mother and siblings. Her mother and Bernice would often come to visit her. Edith missed her siblings deeply and would take a bus to visit Ruth and Reginald (Buck). Ruth and Buck were being raised by separate families. Lila developed some resentment toward Bernice for spending money on Edith. She thought it as unfair to the other children living at the house.

During the seventh grade Edith had a frightening experience. Her teacher took the class to the park for a picnic. There was a swimming pond that had a lifeguard. Edith went into the water with the other kids. Edith did not know how to swim and almost drowned. Edith credits the lifeguard for saving her life. Edith continued to live with Lila until she graduated. She then moved to Columbia, South Carolina. She worked a couple jobs before going into nursing school in Spartanburg, South Carolina.

While in nursing school, the students were invited to attend a military dance in Spartanburg, South Carolina. It was at this dance where she met Robert Roe. Robert was in the Army and stationed at Camp Croft in South Carolina. They were married 6 months later on August 8, 1943, at Bethel Methodist church in Spartanburg, South Carolina.

Edith and Robert

2 A NORTHERN BOY FROM BAYFIELD COUNTY

Robert George Roe was born to George and Mabel Roe, on May 13, 1919. He was raised in Iron River, Wisconsin. Iron River is a small town in northern Wisconsin. It rests about 37 miles east of Superior, Wisconsin.

Robert's love of art and wildlife began at a young age.

> Bob Roe was born an artist. Pictures from the back of his mind flowed from the tip of his pencil. He could draw before he could write. His teachers encouraged him, and his neighbors in rural Bayfield County would look up and say, 'There goes Bobby with his dog and his sketch pad,' and go about their business (Sprain, 1990).

He would spend a lot of time in the outdoors observing wildlife, which he would then turn into a picture. "I'd go out and sit on the bank of the creek and watch the fish, the beavers, and the muskrats. I just loved the outdoors. Sometimes I'd stay all night" (Sprain, 1990).

Robert enlisted in the Army in 1942. He was stationed at Camp Croft in South Carolina. While in the Army, Robert was an ammunition inspector. He inspected mortar shells to find defects in workmanship. Robert also was a sign painter. He worked on posters, metal street signs and building numbers. He was also a cartoonist for the Stars and Stripes and Yank magazines. Robert would eventually work as a commercial artist at ABC Outdoor Advertising, which he did for 33 years. He painted the large billboards that are along highways. It is amazing to think that at one time those billboards were all painted by hand. That's definitely talent and hard work. Robert was very loyal to his job. He never took a day off, even when he was sick. He would have to work in all types of conditions. He had injured himself at times from falls from the scaffolding. Despite the falls and injuries, he continued to work so that he could provide for his family. He would eventually injure his back from a fall which would convince him to retire.

3 TRAIN RIDE TO IRON RIVER

Robert and Edith's first child was Ronald Van Roe (he would be referred to as, "Van") who was born on April 13, 1944. It was decided that Edith would take Van to Iron River, Wisconsin, before Robert was discharged from the Army. She boarded the train and headed north. "I felt some fear because it was during the war and there were a lot of servicemen on the train." She had to switch trains in Chicago. While in the process, her luggage bag fell open. A kind soldier came and helped her pick up the luggage. The train then headed to Superior, Wisconsin. It was a long trip. "I thought I would never get there." It was also during the winter time. Edith had never been this far north and was not used to this type of weather. As she was traveling north the snow on both sides of the train began to get taller and taller. "I began to panic, I thought I was in Alaska." Robert's mother Mabel, and brother, Georgie, met her at the train station. They took Edith and bought her a winter coat along with winter clothes for Van.

Robert was honorably discharged from the Army on January 27, 1945. Robert joined Edith in Iron River. They lived with Robert's parents, George and Mabel until they could find their own home. They finally found a place to rent. Survival was tough during that time, just like it was for most people. Neighbors helped each other out. There were times when Edith would have to ask her neighbors for food. She would also do the same to help a neighbor in need.

One day Edith went to look for Van. Van had gotten into Robert's paints. She found Van with the neighbor boy, David. David was naked and painted green. This would be an early start on Van's mischievous behaviors, which he would be known for.

While in Iron River, Robert and Edith had four more children. Their second child, Robert Jr., was born on April 27, 1945. Robert Jr. was born prematurely and would need a blood transfusion. Edith provided her own blood for the transfusion. Their third child was Edith (referred to as "Sister") who was born on June 14, 1946. Their fourth child was Reginald who was born on June 21, 1947. Their fifth child was Roger who was born on July 23, 1948.

Life was not easy living in Iron River. There were more job opportunities elsewhere. In 1950, Robert accepted the job at ABC Outdoor Advertising in Pewaukee, Wisconsin. Pewaukee, at that time, was a small town (population was 1,792). Pewaukee rests 17 miles west of Milwaukee. It took many hours to get to Pewaukee from Iron River. All the children sat in the bed of the pick-up truck. On the way down they went through a town that was having a parade. Aunt Shirley (Robert's sister) made all the children wave. People thought they were part of the parade.

In Pewaukee, Robert had purchased a small, two-bedroom cottage home on Ash Street. He did this without involving Edith in the decision. Edith wanted to cry because of the smallness of the home. Many memories would be made in that small home on Ash Street. Two more children were born to Robert and Edith while living in Pewaukee. Their sixth child was Royce who was born on May 22, 1950. Their seventh and last child was Rodney who was born on May 31, 1953.

Edith and Van

4 A SON'S ILLNESS

Roger was a very smart child. He was very good at putting puzzles together. One day at breakfast time, Robert's brothers Georgie and Leonard were present. Someone asked Edith what she was making Roger for breakfast. She spelled it out to them "E-G-G". Roger said, "I don't want any damn egg."

Prior to moving to Pewaukee, all the children had the chicken pox. Roger only had a few spots on him. It was after this that he started to become ill. Roger was diagnosed with Bright's disease, a condition where the kidneys become inflamed. Blood and proteins then leak into the urine. It can occur after certain infections. There was a belief that the chicken pox had settled in his kidneys.

Bobby remembers, "I always picture Roger looking at me from his crib and asking me if he could have some fig newton cookies. Those were his favorites. I gave him some and the next day his eyes were swollen shut and his face and joints were all swollen." This was a symptom of the Bright's disease.

Roger's illness was progressively getting worse. After moving to Pewaukee they consulted with a doctor who was just starting his practice in Waukesha. The doctor would come to the house to check on Roger. He would also check the rest of the kids. Roger eventually went to live with his grandparents, George and Mabel, who were living in Waukesha because Roger required a lot of care. This allowed Robert and Edith to focus on the other children. Bernice had even offered to take the rest of the children so Robert and Edith could care for Roger. Edith declined her offer. The doctor stated there was nothing that he could do but that they were doing research in Chicago. Roger was five years old at the time. He was admitted to Passavent Hospital in Chicago, Illinois.

Robert and Edith could not come to visit as much as they wanted to. "I didn't get down there to visit Roger as much as I would have liked to because of the other children I had to raise. I also didn't have a driver's license and Robert had to provide an income."

Roger was there for three weeks before he died on February 26, 1953, at Passavent Hospital. The day before he died, Edith was able to visit him. Edith stated,

> We thought he would make it. I was in disbelief. What bothered me the most was not being there to say good-bye to him, and being alone in a strange place. But he knew I loved him. I grieved privately. Only God knew what was in my heart and the buckets of tears I shed.

Since then there is an increased understanding of

the disease and physicians are able to prescribe the right type of treatment. The prognosis is a lot better then what it was in 1953.

Roger is standing in the front. The second row from left to right is Bobby, Sister and Reggie. In the back row is cousin Barbara and Van.

5 SISTER'S SHADOW

Edith was pregnant with her seventh child at the time of Roger's death. Rodney was born on May 31, 1953. Money was tight. Edith started working as a nurse's aide when Rodney was an infant. She worked the third shift. She would come home and make sure the kids got off to school on time. She would then watch Rodney because they couldn't afford a sitter. The only time she could nap was when he was sleeping. She would then have to make dinner for the family. The people she worked with were very under- standing. They would cover for her and let her go into one of the empty rooms and sleep if needed. She eventually went back to school and became a Licensed Practical Nurse. She worked many years at Northview Home in Waukesha which was an institution for the mentally ill.

Rodney developed a special attachment to Sister. Rodney would follow Sister wherever she went. Sister stated, "He was my shadow." He would refer to Sister as "Titer." Rodney also had a neighbor friend by the name of Gail. He had fun playing with Gail. He would take stuff over such as crackers or cereal in his hands and he would say, "Which hand Gail?" He would make sure to grab a graham cracker for Gail when he would go to play with her.

Another good memory was when it was Easter and there was a bowl of eggs on the table to be boiled. Rodney decided to have fun and took the bowl of eggs and smashed all the eggs on the table. Sister remembers the Christmas when he received a red fire engine toy. He was so excited about this gift and spent a lot of time playing with it.

Pewaukee Lake was in short walking distance from the home. On a warm summer day, it was normal to go to the lake. On July 18, 1957, all the kids walked down the road to Pewaukee Lake. Rodney was four years old at this time. When it came time to leave, Rodney could not be found. He had last been seen on the pier with Royce. Sister got on her bike and rode home and yelled, "Mom, I can't find Rodney." Sister remembers getting on her bike and riding for miles calling for Rodney. The police became involved and dragged the lake. Four hours later his body was found next to the pier. The thought is that he probably saw something in the water, reached down for it and fell in. Sister came home and crawled underneath her bed. When Edith walked back home there were family members at the house. She walked into the house to find Mabel (Robert's mother) making accusations toward her. "How could Edith let this happen?" "Why wasn't she watching that child?" "It's all her fault." Edith was hurt that everyone was consoling Mabel and it wasn't even her child. Edith went to the back porch to be alone. Sister, along with her neighbor, Dorothy, went outside to console her.

The next day the funeral director stopped by the house to drop off Rodney's clothes. Sister was at home at the time. The clothes included Rodney's blue shorts and navy blue and white striped shirt. Edith was in shock. She took them down to the burning barrel and lit a fire. She burned the clothes and cried. Edith stated,

> When I lost Rodney I became angry and it took a long time to get over it. I put the blame on me. After some time had passed I said to myself, 'I was a good mother to him, loved him and gave all I had to him.' I accepted it as an accident which it was, but made the wrong choice for him, and we all make wrong choices, human nature. Someday I will understand God's plans.

Several years after Rodney's death; Sister, was awakened during the night by someone saying "Titer," "Titer." It was Rodney sitting by her bed in a bright radiant glow. Frightened, she pulled the covers over her head. Sometimes God allows things like this to happen to us. It was as though God was saying, "He is okay, he is in my hands."

Sister, Gail and Rodney

6 THE BOY WITH A SMILE

Royce was the boy with a smile. Edith describes his smile as "a smile that would have charmed a lion." Sister stated, "Royce was our baby brother. There wasn't anything each of us would not have done for him. We all thought for Royce. I believe he was in third grade before he learned to tie his shoes. We did it for him." Van was Royce's idol. Van could do anything to Royce and Royce would never retaliate. Royce had a fondness for the outdoors just like Van did. Hunting and fishing were hobbies of Royce's. There was even a picture of Royce in the Pewaukee paper holding two northern pike that he caught in Pewaukee Lake. Uncle Leonard (Robert's brother) would often take Royce and his brothers hunting.

It was no surprise that Royce showed interest in joining the Marines. He wanted to follow in Van's footsteps. Royce talked with a recruiter but because he was seventeen he would need his parent's signature to enlist. Robert and Edith refused to sign. Royce asked Sister if she could talk them into signing. Sister agreed to under conditions that he would get his GED while in the service and learn a trade while he was in the service or once he got out. Sister talked with their parents and also had Royce talk to them about his plans after the service. Robert and Edith agreed with these promises and signed the paperwork. There was worry though, with the Vietnam War being fought.

Royce enlisted and was sent to San Diego where he completed basic training. He was then sent to Vietnam. He was a part of the third battalion, 12th Marines. He was stationed in Quang Tri Province. His battalion was in charge of fire support for the Neville Base. It was a base that was carved out of mountainous terrain. It was about the size of a football field. The ground was very rocky and often had low-lying clouds.

> Captain John E. Knight, Jr., commanding Hotel Company, described the early morning hours of 25 February 1969 as a typical night at FSB Neville. It was, he said, 'very foggy; it looked like something right out of a horror movie with fog drifting through the trees; visibility almost nil. The first indication we had that anything was out of the ordinary other than just normal movement was when a trip flare went off. Neville was under attack by some 200 sappers from the 246th NVA regiment.' According to Sergeant Terry Webber, 'The earth trembled and the noise was deafening. I felt as if the world was ending that foggy night' (Crumley, p.3).

The NVA finally retreated. Royce lost his life in this battle along with 13 other men. He died instantly of multiple shrapnel wounds to the body. With respect and honor, I will list the men that gave their lives that day.

HM2 Walter P. Seel, Moorestown, NJ

Cpl Jeffery M. Barron, LA Puente, CA

LCpl Thomas H McGrath, Homewood, IL

Cpl Gerald D. Zawadzki, Brooklyn, OH

LCpl Steven V. Garcia, Phoenix, AZ

HM3 John M. Sullivan, El Cajon, CA

PFC Raymond L. Flint, Skaneateles, NY

PFC Walter L. Lamarr, Sturtevant, WI

PFC Samuel C. Macon, Delray Beach, FL

PFC David A. Mallory, Huntsville, AL

PFC Royce E. Roe, Pewaukee, WI

PFC Carey W. Smith, Doraville GA

PFC Willie F. Smith, Houston TX

PFC Michael L Zappia, Des Moines, IA

Van received a letter in the mail dated March 25, 1969, from 1st Platoon Commander Terrance Clark describing the battle. The letter went as follows.

Early in the morning of February 25, fire base support base Neville was overrun by a force of elite North Vietnamese assault troops which was backed by an infantry force of undetermined size. The main force of the attack fell on the portion of the lines manned by the 1st Platoon Hotel Company. The attack was quick and violent but failed because the individual Marines of the platoon fought with the fierce professional pride that has become a tradition in the Corps. However, the attack was so bold that many men were forced to give their lives in defense of the others on the hill and in defense of peace and freedom. Your brother was among these brave young men. May God's blessings be with them all.

Edith had recently got home from the funeral of her sister, Ruth, in South Carolina. Bobby was sleeping because he was working nights. Edith was on the phone talking to Mabel. There was a knock on the door. She told Mabel, "just hold on, there's someone at the door, it's probably a salesman."

At the door were two fully dressed Marines. Her thought was that they must be friends of Royce's and were coming to visit. These two men were there to inform her that her son, Royce, had died. Edith screamed, "Oh my God, Oh my God, it's Royce, it's Royce." Edith went to Bobby and said "Bobby, Bobby, get up, it's Royce, he's dead." Edith collapsed into

Bobby's arms. Edith told Bobby, "You have to go tell your dad." The next day Edith told everyone that they needed to go back to work. It would be a couple weeks before the body came back. As they were preparing the funeral, Van asked a friend, Tommy, to sing "Precious Lord Take My Hand," and the "Battle Hymn of the Republic." Tommy had a voice like Elvis.

After the funeral Van talked to one of the Marines who had come to the door. The Marine came up to Van because they knew he had served in the Marines. He said, "I've been doing this and it's hard to tell these parents but when your mother came to that door I knew then this was going to be one of the hardest ones. There was just something about her that just touched my heart." Edith stated,

> You would have loved Royce, big brown eyes and a smile that would have charmed a lion. Each day he was oversees I prayed for him. When we received the news, I was angry at God. With His power, how could He do that to me? So many young boys like him lost their lives; 58,000. I had just returned from South Carolina from my sister's funeral. I don't recall a lot that took place, I was numb. I often think and am heartbroken that I couldn't help the other children with their grief. I'm sure that they have forgiven me.

There was a week after Edith retired and was living in Montello where she felt Royce's presence wherever she went. Edith had Royce on her mind all week. "I just felt that every move that I made he was right next to me." She sat in a chair one day and closed her eyes. She had a dream that he kissed her on the cheek. She stated that she woke up and her cheek was wet.

A Pewaukee High School teacher, Dick Opie, talks about a trip he took to Washington D.C in the <u>Lake County Reporter</u>. Dick stated,

> Some paid dearly with lost fingers, torn backs, or agent orange ingestion. One paid the ultimate sacrifice. He happened to be one of those guys who always had a smile for everyone. On Feb.25, 1969, at age 18, he stopped smiling. When we got to the Vietnam Wall Memorial we found black granite in two halves each 247 feet long. One pointed to the Washington Monument and the other to the Lincoln Memorial. There are over 58,000 names of American service personnel, all casualties of the war. Each name is inscribed in the granite in chronological order of when each person became a casualty. Thus, the names would become the memorial. I became overawed at the silence and the immensity of those names at the wall. The National Park Service has a guide stationed next to the

memorial, so I went over and inquired how I could find the name of this former student on the memorial. The lady at the desk asked me his name and fed it into a computer. In a few seconds she tore off a sheet of paper and asked, 'Is his hometown Pewaukee Wisconsin?' Just as she said this, she looked up and saw my sweatshirt which had 'Pewaukee Pirates' on it. She then said, 'This must be him!' She handed me two sheets of paper and a large pencil. 'When you find his name, you can trace it off the wall and onto this paper.' The other paper said:

Last name: Roe

Given name: Royce Evert

Rank: PFC

Branch of service: Marine Corps

Birthday: 22 May 50

Casualty day: 25 Feb. 69

Hometown of record, Pewaukee, Wis.

Panel 31W; line number 056.

I took the paper and went down to the wall and found Royce's name and then as tears came to my eyes and a lump formed in my throat, I carefully traced his name. Now when Memorial Day comes or when I hear the Star Spangled Banner being played at a ball game, I stand a little taller, stretch a little straighter, and press my hand a little tighter to my heart. An extra tear comes to my eyes as I remember the guy who always had a smile on his face as well as those others who gave of themselves so we could all stand in freedom of mind, body, heart and soul (p.24).

On March 17th, 1969, Robert went before the Pewaukee town board. He asked for their approval to erect a memorial in Royce's name at West Park (name has since changed to Nettesheim Park). Permission was granted. Royce was the only service man in Pewaukee that died in the war. There were donations that provided for a memorial to be placed at the park. A friend of Royce's built the memorial. On June 14th the memorial was unveiled. The memorial is still in the park to this day.

I want to conclude this chapter with a poem that Bobby wrote, called "For my brother."

FOR MY BROTHER

Young boy left home,

Not to roam.

But to fight a war

On a distant shore.

A young man came home,

Not to roam.

Not to boast or brag;

But, in a body bag.

So I can live in the land of the free.

For how many years,

Will mothers shed tears?

For boys who leave home,

Not to roam.

But to fight a war,

On a distant shore.

So I can live in the land of the free.

Memorial Day is a special day for me.

For I have a brother who, went across the sea.

To fight a war,

On a distant shore.

He left his dad and mom

To fight a war in Vietnam.

He did come home,

Not to roam.

Not to boast or brag.

He came home in a body bag.

So I can live in the land of the free.

Today as the flags fly,

And the parades pass by;

I say a silent prayer,

To my God who is always there.

Thank You, for those who paid the price.

Those who gave the ultimate sacrifice.

Thank You, for those who died for me;

So I can live in the land of the free.

Private First Class Royce Roe

Bob standing in front of the memorial that was dedicated to Royce.

7 THE FONZ OF THE FAMILY

Van was always up to something. Reggie stated, "Van was always pulling jokes and pranks with the other kids. I considered him 'the Fonz' of the family." He would get into fights and then be friends with the person the next day. He wasn't a mean person, just mischievous.

Money was limited. The kids had to take turns on the one bike they had. It was Reggie's turn to the ride the red bike. Van, being the oldest, thought he was entitled to ridding it and skipped ahead in the line. Reggie informed Van, "It is my turn." Van hopped on the bike and rode off on it. Reggie hid behind a huge lilac bush and waited for Van to ride by. When Van rode by Reggie ran out with a stick and put it in the spokes of the tire. Van went tumbling off the bike. Reggie grabbed the bike and took off on it. Van went limping home with road rash on his arms and face.

One day while at school Van and his friend Wayne decided to shut the water off to the school. In the boy's bathroom behind the stalls were the valves to turn the water on and off. The only access was through a locked door, or if one was as adventurous as Van, one found another way. The mistake that the boys made was they told others what they did. They attempted a second time and got caught. The school put ink on the valves. Busted! Once found out, they were suspended for three days, with no make-up in school assignments. Van and Wayne had a contest going as to who could fail the most subjects. It was likely a tie. There was an incident when Van and a friend of his decided as a joke to shave their eye brows off. He was always doing something.

Reggie remembers a situation where he became angry at Van. Reggie and a friend of his raised three muscovy ducklings. They were named Huey, Dewey and Louie. One day Reggie came home from Cub Scouts and Royce and Van had him come to the back porch. Royce smiled and said, "Go look on the garage door." There hung Huey, Dewey, and Louie with their heads chopped off. Royce said, "Van did it." The neighbors were complaining about them pooping all over the yard. Reggie stated, "I was so angry with Van that I chased him though the house, grabbed a broom and threw it at him. He ducked and it went right into the wall." That Sunday mom cooked the ducks for dinner. George and Mabel were invited for dinner. Prayer was said and it came time to eat. Reggie's friend Bernie was present. Bernie asked mom, "Which one is Huey? Which one is Dewey? Which one is Louie?" Reggie stated, "We all started crying and dinner had to wait awhile."

Van joined the Marines. One evening during boot camp he had an experience similar to what Sister had with Rodney. He woke up with his name being called, "Van, Van." At the foot of his bunk stood Roger, with a glow of light around him. Van became frighten and pulled his covers over his head. Van completed boot camp and was then stationed at Guantanamo Bay. This was during the Cuban Missile Crisis.

Van married Linda. Linda was from South Carolina just like Edith was. Van and Linda had a daughter named Theresa. They resided in Oconomowoc, Wisconsin. Van was employed as a police officer.

Nine months later after the death of Royce, Sister got a call at work from Edith. She said, "Can you come home? Van didn't come home from bowling last night." Sister replied, "I'll be home." Sister and Edith got in the car and drove over to Oconomowoc to where Van and his wife, Linda were living. In the meantime, Linda was calling all over to see where Van was. Nobody knew. Theresa, just got up from her nap and everyone was about to walk out the door when the phone rang. It was the coroner. Linda collapsed. Edith then got on the phone and he told her that they found Van's body. He missed a curve on his way home and went down an embankment, flew out of the car and the car rolled on top of him. He died instantly according to the coroner.

In her grief, Edith sat on the couch and said, "Oh God, God don't take any more of my children." She cried, "God please take me, don't do this to me any-more God. Are you going to take all my children from me, what have I done!" Edith stated, "but this was an accident also."

They all got in the car and headed back to Pewaukee. Before heading back Edith called and talked to Bobby. She said, "Bobby go tell your Dad, go get your Dad." Judy (Reggie's wife) and her father went to tell Reggie at work.

Christmas of 1969 was very sad. Things weren't the same. The loss of both Royce and Van in the same year made the grief very difficult. Shortly after Christmas, Linda and Theresa moved to South Carolina. Edith stated, "I have always lived with the fear of the loss of the three that are left. I never got to say good-bye to the ones I lost."

Van

8 WALKING ON PINS AND NEEDLES

There was another issue in the Roe home that made things difficulty. Robert struggled with alcoholism and would often become abusive when he drank. His alcohol use progressed over time. It was normal for Robert to get off work at 3:30 pm and not be home until 6:00 pm. He would stop at bars on the way home. At times Robert would become physically and emotionally abusive to Edith and the kids.

Sister remembers coming home one time after work. The phone rang and it was Edith. She said, "Where is he?" Sister replied, "He is sleeping." She stated that she was at the neighbor's house and asked sister if she could bring some clothes over for her. Sister walked to the neighbor's house. Edith had been beat up by Robert. She spent a couple days at the neighbor's house.

As the boys got older he knew not to touch her. The boys would stand up to Robert as they got older. There was a day when one of the boys came home from rabbit hunting. Edith would always soak the rabbits they shot in water. Robert came home that day drunk, picked up the rabbit and threw it at her. That was the last time he did anything because one of the boys stepped in and shoved him.

The physical and emotional abuse of the children eventually stopped as they got older and would be able to stand up for themselves.

Edith would cope by distancing herself from Robert through work, friends, church, volunteering and organizations such as Gold Star Mothers. She surrounded herself with positive supportive people.

People have asked her why she stayed in the marriage. Her reasoning is she had nowhere to go. Back then there weren't the domestic violence shelters like there are now. Women in these relationships often feel stuck. Some women are made to feel by their abuser that they can't survive without them. Some women have a hard time leaving because of the threat of the abuser harming them or the children.

Robert tried to make up for the hurt he caused his family by having a good relationship with his grandchildren. As his grandson, I have pleasant memories of him and the time he spent with me. Memories of canoeing, fishing and driving around in the evening to the count the deer in the field. He was always there for me in good and bad. I remember going through a difficult time in my life when I was attending college at Southwest Baptist University. It was a low point in my life. I was extremely depressed. One day in May, I went to my mail box and inside there was a letter from him. There was a check from him and my grandmother to help me out with bills. In the letter he stated, "I beg of you please don't give up! Be patient, nothing in this world comes easy. Grandma and I had our share of troubles. God tested us too." I immediately saw my grandparent's life behind these words. Nothing came easy for them. I needed to accept this truth into my own life that I too will have hardships and need to work on being more patient with life.

Late in his life, Robert become ill and was taken to the Wisconsin Veteran's Home in King, Wisconsin. Robert's life came to an end on August 20, 2006.

9 BOBBY, REGGIE AND SISTER

The surviving children are Bobby, Reggie and Sister. This chapter is about their grief and what they do to help themselves.

Bobby stated that what has helped him cope is knowing that he will see his brothers again.

> They are all in Heaven! I have that 'blessed hope' that is spoken about in the Bible. Also what has helped is making the choice on how you will let the grief affect your life. In every circumstance of life, we have a choice on how that incident will affect our lives, and the choice is ours. We can make it into a tombstone or a stepping stone. We can live a life that says 'woe is me' or use the test and trials of life to give God glory.

Bobby found a sense of purpose by helping others in their grief. Bobby puts together scrapbooks of poems and literature to give to loved ones who lost someone in the military. "Roe makes the books with no strings attached for fallen soldiers from Oklahoma and Wisconsin, his home state, in part to honor his younger brother who was killed in Vietnam" (Lautenberger). I remember going to one such family when he was visiting me in Green Bay. We arrived at the residence. They received Bobby and I into their home and had a lot to say about their son, Ryan

Jerabek, who served in the Marines. He died in Iraq on April 6, 2004. These parents had also lost their daughter several years prior to an illness.

Reggie remembers asking Edith why Roger and Rodney died. She responded, "God only knows why. Just be strong." It became harder for Reggie to grieve after Royce and Van died in the same year. Reggie stated, "I had trouble believing this had happened. Four brothers gone." He states that Edith told him to be strong and believe in God. Reggie found therapy in the outdoors. He would spend time hunting and fishing with his son and others. Reggie always had a dog. Pets can be very therapeutic with grief.

Sister had a close bond with Edith as she was the only daughter. Sister stated,

> Even though after all these years, I miss them. God is good. He's given me a reminder of each brother through my children and grand-children. Whether it be a little quirk, a facial resemblance, personality, they're there. There have been times I've felt their presence next to me. Also, each day that passes is one more day I'm closer to seeing them, my beautiful mother, and most importantly my Lord Jesus.

Everyone grieves differently. You need to find what works for you. The last chapter talks about some possible coping strategies that might help you.

Bobby, Sister, Reggie (1998)

10 CARING FOR THOSE IN NEED

Edith continued to work at Northview Home doing what she was best at, which was caring for people. Northview Home was an institute for the mentally ill. She eventually retired from there in 1978. Edith told a story about a young man who lived in Pewaukee. He had a troubled life and was sent to Northview Home because of threats he made to harm people. The staff at the home were terrified of him. This man was a friend of Van's and knew Edith. Once he saw Edith he became an entirely different person. She would go out of her way to visit this man when she was working and do little favors for him.

Another story she talked about was in regards to another male patient. Edith stated,

> I was beginning my tour of A.M duty, the phone rang asking me to go over to see Mr. John Doe, he is acting strange. Upon arrival, I found John on his knees on the floor, with lower arms tucked in his axilla saying, 'tweet, tweet, I'm a bird,' continually repeating the same phrase. I must say I did chuckle to myself, but quickly I knew I had to try to reduce his anxiety as he was fantasizing, and his behavior may reflect upon the other unit residents. I heard remarks such as, 'He's crazy,' 'Look, he thinks he's a bird,' 'What's wrong with this man?' My approach was I

stood closely to him, in a soft but firm tone of voice repeated three times, 'You are not a bird, you are John Doe. Please get up.' Finally, he got up from the floor and finished his breakfast.

Edith shared her approaches with others. In a speech at the technical college in 1978 to other LPN's, she talked about ways to address clients. In her speech she talked about the death of a resident who had been there twenty years. She talked about how this affected the residents whether they expressed emotions or not. She shared some advice about helping someone in grief. It was probably spoken from her own grief with losing her sons.

Encourage the individual to talk about their feelings. Spend time, he or she needs someone to listen. Be truthful, supportive, and try to understand how that person may feel. Let them know that there is nothing bad about crying, as the elderly often try to hide their feelings due to the era they grew up in. Just a squeeze of the hand gives a message that someone cares.

She received a letter from her manager after her retirement which stated,

You are gifted with a tremendous ability to be sensitive to the needs and feelings of others;

staff as well as residents. Your willingness to give of yourself without expectations of glory except that which you found within yourself is an attribute that is not found readily in today's society. Your kindness, interest, skill and tact which was so vital in caring for the residents at Northview will be missed. We will remember you and honor you by striving to care for residents by using the gentle, benign, helpful approach you used.

Her life involved caring for others. She saw the good in others. I think this is why people were attracted to her. Bobby stated, "Mom had a way of turning grizzly bears into teddy bears." She was always serving. Always giving. She wouldn't hesitate to help someone in need. It is no surprise that she became a nurse. It was another opportunity to care for others. Edith's granddaughter, Tiffany, became a nurse also. Tiffany stated, "Ever since I was a young girl and saw my grandmother as a nurse, I wanted to become an R.N" (Berlin Journal).

One day a neighbor woman stopped by the house. This woman had eight children and her husband recently left her. She asked Edith if she could have a can of vegetables and toilet paper. Edith's mother, Lottie was also at the home at the time. Edith did not hesitate. She gave this woman what she needed. Afterwards Lottie asked Edith, "How could you do that?" She knew Robert and Edith didn't have much either. She responded. "They have less than we do."

While at Northview she became friends with Nola. This friendship would last to the day that Edith died. Nola stated, "She was my Wisconsin sister, more than a good friend."

11 MOVE TO MONTELLO

Nola and her husband Leo had moved to Montello, Wisconsin, in 1975. Montello is a small town on the Fox River. Within the town there are two lakes, Buffalo Lake and Montello Lake. Robert and Edith would come up to the Wilderness Campground on weekends to camp and spend time with Leo and Nola. The Wilderness Campground was a few miles away from Montello. Leo and Nola would come to the campground to visit. The home across the street from Nola's home came up for sale around 1979. Robert and Edith decided to move to Montello and purchased the home.

This was the right place for them to be. Edith was very active in her church. She would volunteer her time in their thrift store or help out in the children's classes. She also took a job working as a LPN at the Montello Care Center. She put in many hours at the Care Center caring for elderly people. She would one day take her last breath in this facility, probably in a room where at one time she cared for residents. She also continued to volunteer her time at the Wisconsin Veteran's Home in King, Wisconsin. Edith and some friends of hers would make the commute there to help these service men. Helping would involve taking the time to visit. She would bring bakery items and would listen.

One man touched me so, she said. He was blind and had been in the battle of the bulge in WWII. He told me he walked to shore in water that looked like blood. He said you'd stumble over bodies, but keep going, keep going. I've often thought of that, stumbling over your buddy and you can't pick him up. He said the sky looked like it was on fire (McGwin, p.13).

Edith's friend, Nola, helped her cope with her grief throughout the years. "Years ago people did not want to talk to you about death, and that was too bad. I always received a lot from talking." She confided in her friend Nola. Nola stated, "she suffered all loses deeply." Nola was always the driver since Edith didn't drive. They were always getting lost. Nola stated that this is a favorite memory. "Getting lost with her whenever we went somewhere and her witty comments after stopping 50 times for directions to go less than five miles from our destination."

Robert and Edith would finish their lives living in Montello.

.

Packy Wacky Red Hatters outing. Edith is in front and Nola is in the back.

12 GOLD STAR MOTHER

Elissa Kaupisch in her article, <u>Blue Star Tradition Dates Back to World War I</u> talks about the origins of the Gold Star Mothers.

> In June 1928, Grace Darling Seibold of Washington, D.C., who lost a son in World War I, founded American Gold Star Mothers for the purpose of supporting a group of mothers who had lost sons and daughters during the war. In January 1929, the non-profit, patriotic organization incorporated. The group's purpose was to perpetuate the ideas of Americanism for which service members had fought and died (Vol. 79, No.2).

Edith belonged to the Gold Star Mothers. She was often asked to speak at events. She was involved in a Memorial Service event in Oshkosh in 2002. Here is an excerpt from the Oshkosh Northwestern.

> 'They are gone from our lives, but not from our hearts,' she said. 'We have many fond memories of him, and good memories never die.' Roe said the Gold Star Mothers are a reminder that freedom is not free. 'Just think of all the lives and sacrifices given,' she said. 'It's the price we've had to pay for freedom' (p. A6).

Another such event was the following Memorial Day, 2003, in Montello, WI. Her message was as:

Welcome veterans, guests, visitors and Montello citizens. On behalf of all the Gold Star Mothers. Thank you for showing your patriotism by being here on this Memorial Day of 2003. We are here to pay homage to those who have given their lives for their country and flag. It is in these moments with sadness and pride, that we remember those who died to keep this nation's freedom. It is a time of renewal for all of us. A Gold Star Mother or Dad are the parents of a son or daughter who gave their life serving the military. President Woodrow Wilson said, the term Gold Star Mother, signifies not only a young life given in service to America, but the pride, dignity, and devotion to that young American. Our purpose is to assist Veterans and their dependents whenever possible. At this time, we now have lost a young Marine from Beaver Dam. I ask you to keep this family in your prayers as it is a stressful time for the family.

Edith had the opportunity to attend the LZ Lambeau event in May, 2010, in Green Bay, WI. She did not have a lot of mobility and had to be in a wheel chair. She was part of the motorcycle parade so she had to first go to Appleton.

It was in Appleton that she first fell into the loving arms of so many Vietnam veterans and where they helped her onto a motorcycle behind another Vietnam warrior, so that she could ride into Green Bay in a thunder of engines with flags waving and people cheering (McGwin, p.13).

She was driven up from Appleton on the back of a Harley Davidson. The roaring sound of the motorcycles could be heard from a distance. The motorcycle parade was a sight to see as they turned onto Lombardi Avenue and headed toward Lambeau Field.

'This is why they did this,' said the soft spoken 88-year-old Edith. 'They wanted to say thanks. When they came home, they were called baby killers and people spit on them. They tore flags down, our own people. They did (L.Z. Lambeau) to get those feelings healed and I think it did.' (McGwin, p.13)

Being a Gold Star Mother was so important to her that at her funeral she was dressed in her Gold Star uniform. During her wake there was a line of Gold Star Mothers who walked in together to pay their respects.

Edith is in the wheel chair. This picture was taken with her and other Gold Star Mothers at LZ Lambeau in 2010. This was held at Lambeau Field, in Green Bay, Wisconsin.

Edith on the back of a motorcycle

13 PRECIOUS LORD TAKE MY HAND

Edith's life came to an end on August 4, 2012. She died at a nursing home that she used to work at, in a room where she likely spent time caring for residents.

During the wake the door of the funeral home opened and in walked a pre-session of Gold Star Mothers. They walked in a line up to her casket and placed a rose on her. Edith and other Gold Star Mothers were family. They shared a common bond.

After the wake everyone went home to get rest. While sleeping Reggie had a dream of Edith standing at his bedside. Edith stated, "I am safely home." Edith is at home with her boys. The boys she never got to say, "good-bye" to.

At her graveside service, I gave a message out of the Gospel of John. I also had the special privilege of playing my guitar and singing a song, "Precious Lord." This song was sung at the funerals of Royce and Van.

Elvis Presley sings this song on one of his gospel albums. The song was written by Thomas Dorsey (July 1, 1899- Jan 23, 1993). He has been referred to as the father of black gospel music. His wife Nettie died during childbirth in 1932. Two days later, his newborn son also died. In his grief he wrote this song. This song may be your own prayer. Invite the Lord to take your hand. Ask Him to walk with you on your journey through grief.

PRECIOUS LORD

Precious Lord, take my hand

Lead me on, help me stand

I am tired, I am weak, I am worn

Through the storm, through the night

Lead me on to the light

Take my hand, Precious Lord, lead me home

When my way grows drear

Precious Lord, linger near

When my life is al-most gone

Hear my cry, hear my call

Hold my hand lest I fall

Take my hand, precious Lord, lead me home

When the darkness appears

And the night draws near

And the day is past and gone

At the river I stand

Guide my feet, hold my hand

Take my hand, precious Lord, lead me home

14 FAITH, HOPE AND LOVE

I was asked to give the eulogy at my grandmother's funeral. In preparation there were three words that came to my mind: faith, hope and love. I was reminded of the scripture verse. "And now these three remain: faith, hope and love. But the greatest of these is love" (1 Corinthians 13:13, NIV).

My grandmother's Christian faith and her children provided her with reason and hope to endure. "The world keeps turning, regardless of your hardships (seems as if some have more than others) but you must have to have something to grasp for, mine was my faith and my children." A verse that helped her was Philippians 4:8. She wrote this verse out and gave it to me. "Fix your thoughts on what is good and right. Think about things that are pure and lovely, and dwell on the fine, good things in others. Think about all you can praise God for and be glad about it." This is exactly what she did. She focused on what was right and good in her life. She dwelled on what she could praise God for. She had love for others and saw the good in them and spent her life helping others. This, in return, helped her. Edith stated,

> I had no guilt feelings, I put my children first and gave my best to them, never were mistreated, did not have much money but had lots of love for them. My faith and prayers pulled me through. I still believe in prayer as

some of mine have been answered.

Several nieces and nephews would refer to her as "Saint Edie." Her faith in Christ was challenged through the death of her sons. She talked about feelings of anger that she had toward God. Instead of running from God, which many people might do, she did the opposite, she ran to God. It was ultimately God who gave her peace to deal with the grief and to find the acceptance that she needed to move on. Bobby stated,

> Her faith was her source of strength that enabled her to get through all the trials that she faced and be a positive influence for so many others. My mom did not verbalize her faith; she lived it. She made sure we went to church every Sunday and we were involved in as many church activities as she could arrange to get us to.

Reggie talks about his own trouble after the death of Royce and Van and losing them in the same year. Having now lost four brothers. He remembers Edith stating, "Be strong and believe in God. He has the answers." My grandmother did this. It was her prayers that pulled her through like she said.

My grandmother's life was a life of hope. She never gave up. She persevered to the end. Some of you who are reading this may be feeling like giving up and throwing in the towel. Please don't. My grandmother found reason to live. There was a time when she walked across a bridge in Waukesha and had a thought of jumping. A voice inside of her reminded her of her surviving children. "I still have three children that need to be raised." God does have a purpose for you. There will always be a new day, which is what my Grandmother would say. Also learn to be grateful for what you do have. It's easy to look at everything that is wrong with your life. Ask yourself, what is right about it?

My grandmother's life was a life of love. She was always serving and always giving. She didn't have a lot of money to give her children. She had a lot of love. She had a lot of love for her grandchildren also. It doesn't surprise me that she chose to become a nurse. It was another way to love others. In doing so I think it helped her with her own grief and pain. She never wanted people to feel sorry for her. I don't think a lot of people even knew the amount of grief she experienced in her life.

She would always take the time for anyone. She would get calls from people asking for her counsel on their problems. Bobby stated, "It seems that mom always had a tender spot in her heart for others. Most of our friends realized this. They would come to the "Roe house," hungry for food or a kind word and they would find what they were looking for because mom was sensitive to their needs."

A neighbor man was off work for a while recovering from an injury. His favorite thing to do was watch the Roe house in the morning when it was time for the school bus to come. He said he could see the sides of the house swelling up as just about every kid in the neighborhood gathered there to wait for the bus. When the bus arrived he stated that it was like somebody stepped on an anthill. Kids would come running out of that house in every direction. Sometimes it reminded him of one of the fireworks that goes off and fills the air with different colors.

To conclude this chapter, I would like to share a poem that Bob wrote titled, "No sad tears." He wrote this poem in memory of my grandmother.

NO SAD TEARS

Don't shed no sad tears for me.

I'm where I've been longing to be.

I'm at home with Jesus and my boys.

For many long years,

I've shed silent tears

Pining for my boys who went away;

Brokenhearted, over the good-byes, I didn't have a chance to say.

Don't shed no sad tears for me.

I'm where I've been longing to be.

I'm at home with Jesus and the boys.

The instant my heart stopped beating

There was a beautiful meeting.

Jesus and Robert came to greet me.

Jesus was the first one to meet me.

As Jesus held me in his loving embrace;

A mischievous smile came across His face.

He said: "I've been waiting a long time for you."

Others have been waiting a long time too."

Then he smiled wide; as he stepped aside,

And into my arms ran:

Roger, Rodney, Royce, and Van.

Don't shed no sad tears for me.

I'm where I've been longing to be.

I'm at home with Jesus and the boys.

Soon your time down there will be through.

We'll be waiting here in Heaven for you.

Jesus, Me, Robert, and the boys,

Roger, Rodney, Royce and Van

15 COPING WITH GRIEF

I have had the wonderful opportunity to work with Native American people during my employment with the Oneida Nation. Native American history is full of grief and trauma. Native Americans often describe things in circles which implies balance. One circle which you might have heard of is called the "medicine wheel." The authors of the book called <u>The Sacred Tree</u> help to define this.

> The medicine wheel teaches us that we have four aspects to our nature: the physical, the mental, the emotional, and the spiritual. Each of these aspects must be equally developed in a healthy, well-balanced individual through the development and use of volition (i.e. will) (p. 12).

For wellness to occur we must work on the whole person which includes your physical self, emotional self, mental self, and spiritual self. All areas of self are affected by grief. I encourage you to take a piece of paper and list each area, then under each area put down what you are going to do to help yourself. I have listed some examples.

Physical

Grief can take its toll on the body. The other areas of self are affected when you stop taking care of your physical self. It is important that you take care of your body.

1. Make sure you are eating. When people are sad they have a tendency to either not eat or eat too much. Are you are eating the right foods? What you eat can have a big impact on your energy and mood.

2. Make sure you are getting enough rest. How are you sleeping? Is it too much or too little? Find the right balance for yourself. It's hard to cope if you are constantly tired.

3. Make sure you are getting some exercise. When we are sad we often don't want to do anything. Sometimes we need to force ourselves to get some exercise. Find an exercise that works for you. Exercise has been referred to as an anti-depressant as it can release some of feel good chemicals in our body.

4. Make sure you are taking care of any health conditions you have. There are health conditions that have a tremendous impact on your ability to cope if they aren't managed properly.

Emotional

Your emotional self has to do with your feelings. There are many different emotions a person may experience in grief. Some include mad, sad, glad, afraid, ashamed and hurt.

1. Accept your feelings. They are a part of you. The feelings you are experiencing are normal to the grief process. You're not going crazy as you may think. Journaling your thoughts and feelings has been helpful to some people. There's something powerful about writing your thoughts and feelings down.

2. Allow yourself to grieve. It is the result of deep love. When we choose to love someone deeply it is only normal that we would grieve when they are gone. This means feeling and experiencing all the emotions that come with grief. It is normal to feel sad, angry, guilt, lonely, worried, afraid etc. Allow yourself to cry. This is the body's way of releasing the pain. There will be grief triggers. This could be anything from people talking to you about your loved one, a picture, a song, a place or a certain day on the calendar. Allow yourself to have your grief moment.

3. Write a grief letter to your loved one. Find the right time and place to read it to your loved one. Martha Felber talks about this in her book.

   Did you have time to say good-bye to your loved one? Even if you did, are there things you wish you had said? One very helpful way to deal with the things left unsaid is to write a letter to your loved one. Write what you appreciate about your love done. What will you remember? How was your life made better by your loved one being part of it? Pour out your longings and your love. (Felber, p. 76).

4. Share your feelings with someone. The best way to release them is to talk to someone. Share it with those who are supportive. Someone said, "Grief shared is better than grief shouldered." It is important to have supports. June Kolf lost her husband, Jack to cancer. In her book she stated,

> Grief is a heavy burden that can seem back breaking, but a heavy load of any type will seem lighter when it is shared with a friend. I believe God has very large, strong shoulders. He will gladly help carry our load of grief if only we are willing to not clutch it so tightly (Kolf, p.15).

Work on loosening your grip on the pain and talk to someone. As a professional counselor I can't share with you how many times I have counseled people and I didn't say much. I would have people leave the session and they would say that it felt good. All I did was listen. Find someone to listen. The key is supportive people. Don't forget about the story of Job. Job lost his whole family. His friends came and showed no support. They were critical and not understanding. God ended up rebuking these friends (Job 42:7). Find people that are supportive. When I think of support I think of the story of Ruth and Naomi. Naomi lost her husband and two sons. One of her sons was married to Ruth (Ruth 1:3-5). Ruth was a kind person and was determined to not let Naomi be alone (Ruth 1:9, 16, 18). Find a kind person like Ruth to share your grief with.

5. Don't use alcohol and other drugs to cope with grief. Using substances delays the grief and can complicate the process. Substances numb the pain and prevent a person from dealing with the grief. A person can also develop a dependence on substances where they begin to develop high tolerance and a loss of control. Substance use prevents you from coping in a healthy way.

Mental

Your mental self is your thoughts. Our thoughts produce our feelings and behaviors. The acronym, T.E.A. is easy to remember (thoughts = emotions = actions). Are there thoughts or beliefs that are not productive?

1. Think about your loved one more in life then in death. My grandmother focused on the life of her children. She often told stories of when they were alive. You will be lost in sadness if all you focus on is their death or the funeral. Think of good memories and take time to even write them down. Share them with others. My mother always shared stories of her brothers with me and my siblings while we were growing up. I think it helped her in her own grief.

2. Think hopefully. Don't lose hope. Things do have a way of getting better. As I said earlier, my grandmother did have a moment where she thought about taking her life. She found reason and hope. My grandmother continued to live despite the losses of her children. She still had purpose. She would continue to raise the children that remained. She would volunteer her time. She would continue to work. She would spend a lot of time with her grandchildren. Victor Frankl talks about this in his book, <u>Man's Search for Meaning</u>. Victor was a Jewish psychiatrist who was put in the concentration camp along with his wife and family members. He was separated from his family. His parents, his wife and his brother all died in the camp. He found reason to hope. He also taught others in the concentrations camps to do the same. "But I also told them that, in spite of this, I had no intention of losing hope and giving up. For no man knew what the future would bring, much less the next hour (p. 89-90). Victor also went on to say,

> Whoever was still alive had reason for hope, health, family, happiness, professional abilities, fortune, position in society- all these things that could be achieved again or restored. After all, we still had all our bones intact. Whatever we had gone through could still be an asset to us in the future (p. 89).

3. Think like a survivor. Decide that you will live. Don't let death come to your emotional self, physical self, mental self, and spiritual self. Ingrid Trabisch stated, "You don't honor the dead by dying with them." You honor your loved one by choosing to live. I know they would want you to do this.

Spiritual

Your spirit has a lot to do with your personality. It is who you are. How has your personality been affected by grief? Have some of your positive traits disappeared with grief? Have negative traits appeared? Begin to think about ways to bring life back to your spirit. Spiritual practices help to develop our spirit. Allowing the Creator into your life will give peace to your spirit.

1. Invite God into your grief. This may be hard for you to do this. Maybe there is anger that you have toward God. Robert DiGiulio lost his wife, Chrissie and daughter, Christine and his wife's parents in a car accident. In the article, Losing Someone Close, He stated,

> As you struggle to make sense of your tragedy, reassure yourself it's O.K. to be angry with God. But also realize that your loss is not God's punishment or attempt to test you. God shares that hurt in your heart and wants to lead you to new hope and peace.

You have to make the choice. You can either run from God or run to Him. God knows what it is like to grieve. His son died on the cross. Jesus also experienced grief when he walked on this earth. The shortest verse in the bible is "Jesus wept" (John 11:35, NIV). This was after the death of Lazarus. God never promised an easy life. He can provide peace and strength during these times of pain. The prophet Jeremiah was referred to as the weeping prophet. He saw a lot of grief in his life and was also treated unfairly. Jeremiah stated, "O Lord, my strength and my fortress, my refuge in time of distress" (Jeremiah 16:19, NIV).

2. Find some type of meaning. Make the loss stand for something. It's your way of honoring your loved one. My grandmother involved herself with the Gold Star Mother's organization. My grandparents also had a memorial built in remembrance of Royce. Edith would take advantage of speaking opportunities. Allow good things to come from your loss. Life can blossom from death if we allow it. Merton and Irene Strommen talk about the importance of finding significance through their own grief journey. Their son David died at the age of 25. He was working with youth at the time and was struck by lightning.

   Though a foot race may seem insignificant, it is impressive how important the first marathon run for Dave became for me. Its purpose was to raise funds for an endowment established at Augsburg College for training students in youth and family ministry. As I identified with the runners. I felt that something meaningful was being done for an important cause. Standing at various points along the marathon course, I cheered for the eleven red-shirted runners who were running for Dave (p.97).

It doesn't take much to look locally to see an example of this. There is a local charity called, "Colton's Cure." Colton Steinhorst was four years old when he died on September 3, 2013. He lives on through the charity that his parents established. "Colton's Cure Foundation stands to lighten the financial burden of Wisconsin families who are going through a diagnosis of childhood cancer" (www.coltonscure.org).

3. Pray for your loved one. Merton Strommen talks about this. "When I pray for members of my family. I include Dave, asking for his growth and development and that he be informed of our continuing love" (p.53). Praying for loved ones should not stop after they die. We can pray for these things like Merton talks about. A prayer might be something like "Lord, please be with my loved one, remind him/her that we still think often about him/her and that we love him/her greatly."

4. Help someone. Helping others helps yourself. I think my grandmother's service to others helped her through her pain. Find a place where you can volunteer your time. Edith spent numerous hours volunteering herself with church and helping veterans at the Wisconsin Veteran's Home in King, Wisconsin. It also gets you out of the house.

5. Forgive yourself and others. People will hurt you. Edith was hurt by others after Rodney died. She forgave. It is also important to forgive ourselves. It is normal to carry guilt after someone dies. Guilt for something I did or didn't do. Lack of forgiveness keeps you unhappy. You deserve to be happy and free. Set yourself free from resentments. You're only hurting yourself. God tells us to forgive because He forgives. He also tells us to forgive because He knows what is best for us.

6. Find acceptance. It's accepting the loss and any other things that may need to be accepted. Maybe it's accepting that you will not have the answers you need in this lifetime. Another acceptance could be that there was nothing you could have done to stop the death. Maybe its accepting the that the hurt will always be there. Accepting that I can still have life even though I hurt.

7. Have an attitude of gratitude. Are there things you can be grateful for? A person may be grateful for the time they did have with their loved one. Make a list of things that you are grateful for.

8. Give yourself some solitude. It's okay to have some time alone. Even Jesus had to break away from people to be alone. Just don't live in solitude.

9. Simplicity is important. You don't want to take on too much. Taking on too much prevents you from taking care of yourself. Try to find the right balance.

10. Learn to laugh again. Hopefully laughter will return to you. My grandmother was a woman who always had a joke. There was never a shortage of laughter at the Roe house. It became known as the "Roe humor." Bobby stated, "we learned to laugh through our tears". Hopefully your tears will be tears of joy as you reflect on the memories of your loved one. She belonged to a group of women called the "Packy Wacky Red Hatters." She along with other women would go out at times and wear red hats. They would have fun together with a lot of laughter.

The Talking Stick

We all have a story to tell. I shared with you my grandmother's story. What is your story? Native Americans use a talking stick as a way to communicate their story.

These decorated sticks were used during meetings or storytelling to identify the speaker. Whoever held the talking stick was the only person who could speak at that time, while others present had to listen silently and respectfully. When one person was finished speaking, they would pass the stick on, so everyone would have a chance to speak, but one at a time. This ensured that everyone's point of view was heard and considered (Institute for American Indian Studies).

Make your own talking stick. Find a stick or branch. On this stick or branch you will decorate it. Everything you decorate it with should have some type of meaning. Your stick should tell the story of your grief and most of all the things you will do to help yourself with your grief. Some examples of things you could put on your stick could be beads, jewelry, ribbon, cloth, feathers, bells, shells, etc. Be creative. Keep your stick in a place where you can view it frequently. It is a reminder of your story and what you will do to help yourself. Last of all make sure you share your story with someone with the use the talking stick. Use the items you chose to decorate with as the conversation starter.

In conclusion, it is important to seek professional help if needed. There is nothing wrong with asking for help. There are trained counselors who can listen and help you to achieve wellness in these areas of your life. My prayer is that God will comfort you in your grief and that you will find wellness in all areas of your life.

REFERENCES

Colton's Cure- www.coltonscure.org

Crumley, B. 25 February 1969-Fire support bases Neville and Russell. (on-line). Available: www.mca-marines.org/mcaf-blog/2012/02/15/25-february-1969-fire-support-bases-neville-and-russell. 2-4.

DiGiulio, R. (1996). Losing someone close. St. Meinard, IN: Abbey.

Dorsey, T. Precious Lord.

Felber, M. (2000). Finding your way after your spouse dies. Notre Dame, IN: Ave Maria.

Frankl, V.E. (1984). Man's search for meaning: an introduction to logotherapy. (Rev. 3rd ed). New York, NY: Simon & Schuster. 89-90.

The institute for American Indian Studies. (2011). (on-line)Available: http://www.iaismuseum.org/education/teacher-resources/crafts-talking-sticks.pdf

Kaupisch, E. (2002, Feb). Blue star tradition dates back to world war 1. Badger Legionnaire 79, 2

Kolf, J.C. (2001). When will I stop hurting? Grand Rapids. MI. Baker.15

Lane, P, Bopp, J, Bopp, M, & Brown, L. (1984). The sacred tree: Reflections on native American spirituality (4th ed.).Twin Lakes, WI: Lotus.

Lautenberger J. (Aug 24, 2011). Man uses scrapbooks to comfort families of fallen soldiers. (on-line). Available: Tulsaworld.com

McGwin, K. (2010, July 1). A heart of gold in a Gold Star mother. Marquette County Tribune, P. 13.

Opie, D. (1989, June 1). Opie finds real meaning in Memorial day. Lake County Reporter, p.24.

Roe, B. (1993) For my brother.

Roe, B. No sad tears.

Sprain, F. (1990, March 22). Places and faces. The Marquette County Tribune, p.4,

Strommen, M.P, & Strommen, I.A (1996). Five cries of grief: One family's journey to healing after the tragic death of a son. Minneapolis, MN: Augsburg Fortress.

The Bible. The New International Version.

Tiffany Lambert earns scholarship. Berlin Journal.

Zellmer, D. (2002, May 27). Mothers keep memories alive. Oshkosh Northwestern, pp. A1, A6.

ABOUT THE AUTHOR

Tim Lambert lives in Green Bay, Wisconsin. He is married to Cindy and they have two children, Rebekah and Aaron. He received his master's degree from the University of Wisconsin, Oshkosh. He is a Licensed Professional Counselor and a Licensed Clinical Substance Abuse Counselor.

Made in the USA
Middletown, DE
20 February 2021

34127674R00050